The Back Chamber

Poetry by Donald Hall

Exiles and Marriages

The Dark Houses

A Roof of Tiger Lilies

The Alligator Bride

The Yellow Room

The Town of Hill

Kicking the Leaves

The Happy Man

The One Day

Old and New Poems

The Museum of Clear Ideas

The Old Life

Without

The Painted Bed

White Apples and the Taste of Stone

The Back Chamber

THE

BACK

CHAMBER

DONALD HALL

Houghton Mifflin Harcourt
Boston   New York
2011

For information about permission to reproduce selections from this book,
write to Permissions, Houghton Mifflin Harcourt Publishing Company,
215 Park Avenue South, New York, New York 10003.

www.hmhbooks.com

Library of Congress Cataloging-in-Publication Data
Hall, Donald, date.
The back chamber : poems / Donald Hall.
p. cm.
ISBN 978-0-547-64585-8
I. Title.
PS3515.A3152B33 2011
811'.54—dc22

Book design by Greta D. Sibley

Printed in the United States of America

DOC 10 9 8 7 6 5 4 3 2 1

Poems in this book previously appeared elsewhere: *Agni, Amoskeag, The Atlantic
Monthly* ("Goosefeathers," "Alterations," "The Bone Ring," "Blue Snow"),
Arrowsmith Press, Arts and Letters, The Nation, The New Yorker ("Love's Progress,"
"Maples," "Nymph and Shepherd," "Meatloaf" "The Things," "Green Farmhouse
Chairs"), *Onearth, Poetry* ("Convergences," "Advent," "Closing"), *The Threepenny
Review, The Times Literary Supplement, The Sewanee Review,* and *Warwick Press.*

For Deanne Urmy

and

Wendy Strothman

Contents

II. RIC'S PROGRESS

III. ROCKING CHAIRS PAINTED GREEN

I

MEATLOAF

The Things

When I walk in my house I see pictures,
bought long ago, framed and hanging
— de Kooning, Arp, Laurencin, Henry Moore —
that I've cherished and stared at for years,
yet my eyes keep returning to the masters
of the trivial — a white stone perfectly round,
tiny lead models of baseball players, a cowbell,
a broken great-grandmother's rocker,
a dead dog's toy — valueless, unforgettable
detritus that my children will throw away
as I did my mother's souvenirs of trips
with my dead father, Kodaks of kittens,
and bundles of cards from her mother Kate.

Love's Progress

When love empties itself out,
it fills our bodies full.

For an hour we lie twining
pulse and skin together

like nurslings who sigh
and doze, dreamy with milk.

Showtunes

After their tumult, as they quieted,
    She breathed into his ear
    The tunes she loved to sing,
Measuring out the songs of Fred Astaire.
    After she left, he slept
     Deeply, except
To wake from a dream that brought back everything.

Now on the chest of drawers beside the bed
    The candle stays unlit
    That cast its flickering
Over her face as she sighed in wanton secret.
    He cannot go to sleep,
     Needing to keep
His ears tuned to the phone that does not ring.

Ruins

Snow rises as high as my windows. Inside by the fire
my chair is warm, and I remain compounded of cold.

It is unthinkable that we will not touch each other again.

As the barn's bats swoop, vastation folds its wings
over my chest to enclose my rapid, impetuous heart.

It is ruinous that we will not touch each other again.

Ten miles away, snow falls on your clapboard house.
You play with your children in frozen meadows of snow.

Conclusion at Union Lake

We walked in a comfortless quiet
to sit on the shore of Union Lake
an hour in July, as light struck up
white-green from lilypads, motionless

in the steady sun of afternoon,
while loons uncannily wailed
at lake's end, and we watched
mallards drifting two by two.

We sat without speaking, until
the chainsaw rattle of a lightplane
ripped and concluded our silence.
"We'd better be going," she said.

We folded the plaid blanket,
picked up our things, and walked
to the clapboard house, not looking
at the lake we'd never go to again.

Oaks and red maple overhead
gathered as if to consume
our bodies and love into shadow.
There would be no more quarrels.

Three Women

When you like a woman,
you talk and talk.
One night you kiss.
Another night you fuck.
You're both content,
maybe more than content.
Then she goes away.

When you like a woman,
you talk and talk.
One night you kiss.
Another night you fuck.
You're both content,
maybe more than content.
Then she goes away.

When you like a woman,
you talk and talk.
One night you kiss.

Another night you fuck.
You're both content,
maybe more than content.
Then she goes away.

Nymph and Shepherd

She died a dozen times before I died,
And kept on dying, nymph of fatality.
I could not die but once although I tried.

I envied her. She whooped, she laughed, she cried
As she contrived each fresh mortality,
Numberless lethal times before I died.

I plunged, I plugged, I twisted, and I sighed
While she achieved death's paradise routinely.
I lagged however zealously I tried.

She writhed, she bucked, she rested, and, astride,
She posted, cantering on top of me
At least a hundred miles until I died.

I'd never blame you if you thought I lied
About her deadly prodigality.
She died a dozen times before I died
Who could not die so frequently. I tried.

Bangers and Mash

We flew the Atlantic all night, your head
with its first streak of gray leaning
against my shoulder, and took a cab
to our bed-and-breakfast. We napped,
woke up at noon, and rode the tube
from Russell Square to Piccadilly Circus,
where we asked a stranger to take
a photograph of us standing together,
then walked for lunch to the Salisbury,
where in bomb-site London I drank
pints of Younger's before you were born.
Back at the hotel, we made love
as late light slipped through a gap
in the curtains onto your cheekbones,
your nose, your outstanding chin,
and your eyes — dazed like a baby's
sleepy surfeited eyes — that closed
as you said in my ear, "I will lose you."

River

In a dream this August night in St. Petersburg,
I see the years lapse like Cyrillic letters
into the calm and receptive waters of the Neva.

When I was twelve years old in Connecticut,
helmeted soldiers sieging in acres of snow
surrounded Leningrad and the implacable Neva.

They warmed their hands and jackbooted feet
over the gold ashes of Catherine's Palace
inland from the former St. Petersburg's Neva.

Home from eighth grade I read in *Life* how trucks
slipped over frozen Lake Ladoga into the city
and starvation ebbed by the enduring Neva.

When ice melted in the scavenge of Leningrad,
no dogs or cats skittered into ravenous alleys
and squares of ruin beside the relentless Neva.

In St. Petersburg now, reconsecrated St. Isaac's
rises behind the magnanimity of the Hermitage
and boaters drink vodka on the summery Neva.

The Wehrmacht laid siege nine hundred days.
I dream that the years of wasted Leningrad
fall like Cyrillic script into the bounty of the Neva.

Meatloaf

1. Twenty-five years ago, Kurt Schwitters,
I tried to instruct you in baseball
but kept getting distracted, gluing
bits and pieces of world history
alongside personal anecdote
instead of explicating baseball's
habits. I was K.C. (for Casey)
in stanzas of nine times nine times nine.
Last year the Sox were ahead by twelve

2. in May, by four in August—collapsed
as usual—then won the Series.
Jane Kenyon, who loved baseball, enjoyed
the game on TV but fell asleep
by the fifth inning. She died twelve years
ago, and thus would be sixty now,
watching baseball as her hair turned white.
I see her tending her hollyhocks,
gazing west at Eagle Pond, walking

3. to the porch favoring her right knee.
I live alone with baseball each night
but without poems. One of my friends
called "Baseball" *almost* poetry. No
more vowels carrying images
leap suddenly from my excited
unwitting mind and purple Bic pen.
As he aged, Auden said that methods
of dry farming may also grow crops.

4. When Jane died I had constant nightmares
that she left me for somebody else.
I bought condoms, looking for affairs,
as distracting as Red Sox baseball
and even more subject to failure.
There was love, there was comfort; always
something was wrong, or went wrong later
—her adultery, my neediness—
until after years I found Linda.

5. When I was named Poet Laureate,
the kids of Danbury School painted
baseballs on a kitchen chair for me,
with two lines from "Casey at the Bat."
In fall I lost sixty pounds, and lost
poetry. I studied only *Law
and Order.* My son took from my house
the eight-sided Mossberg .22
my father gave me when I was twelve.

6. Buy two pounds of cheap fat hamburger
so the meatloaf will be sweet, chop up
a big onion, add leaves of basil,
Tabasco, newspaper ads, soy sauce,
quail eggs, driftwood, tomato ketchup,
and library paste. Bake for ten hours
at thirty-five degrees. When pitchers
hit the batter's head, Kurt, it is called
a beanball. The batter takes first base.

7. After snowdrifts melted in April,
I gained pounds back, and with Linda flew
to Paris, eating all day: croissants
warm, crisp, and buttery, then baguettes
Camembert, at last boeuf bourguignon
with bottles of red wine. Afternoons
we spent in the Luxembourg Gardens
or in museums: the Marmottan!
The Pompidou! The Orangerie!

8. The Musée de la Vie Romantique!
The Louvre! The d'Orsay! The Jeu de
Paume! The Musée Maillol! The Petit
Palais! When the great Ted Williams died,
his son detached his head and froze it
in a Scottsdale depository.
In summer, enduring my dotage,
I try making this waterless farm,
"Meatloaf," with many ingredients.

9. In August Linda climbs Mount Kearsarge,
where I last clambered in middle age,
while I sit in my idle body
in the car, in the cool parking lot,
revising these lines for Kurt Schwitters,
counting nine syllables on fingers
discolored by old age and felt pens,
my stanzas like ballplayers sent down
to Triple-A, too slow for the bigs.

The Week

There go Monday,
Tuesday, Wednesday . . .
I know their names
from the newspaper
I hold as each day
walks past on Route 4
and stares ahead
no matter high heat
or rain. In winter
sometimes the days
slip on black ice, pick
themselves up
to brush snow off
their gray sweats,
and continue walking
north on blacktop,
each morning
the same but older.

Convergences

At sixteen he dismisses his mother with contempt.
She hears with dread the repulsive wave's approach
and her fifty-year-old body smothers under water.

An old man loses half his weight, as if by stealth,
but finds in his shed his great-grandfather's knobbly cane,
and hobbles toward youth beside the pond's swart water.

She listens to the dun-colored whippoorwill's
three-beat before dawn, and again when dusk
enters the cornfield parched and wanting water.

He imagines but cannot bring himself to believe
that the dead woman enters his house in disguise
or that the young rabbi made *vin rouge* from water.

Within the poem he and she—hot, cold, and luke—
converge into flesh of vowels and consonant bones
or into the uncanny affection of earth for water.

Advent

When I see the cradle rocking
What is it that I see?
I see a rood on the hilltop
    Of Calvary.

When I hear the cattle lowing
What is it that they say?
They say that shadows feasted
    At Tenebrae.

When I know that the grave is empty,
Absence eviscerates me,
And I dwell in a cavernous, constant
    Horror vacui.

Apples Peaches

Apples, peaches,
Pumpkin pie.
How many years
Until I die?

—jump rope rhyme,
A Treasury of New England Folklore

Hostess Twinkies,
Wonder Bread.
How many springs
Until I'm dead?

Plague and pestilence,
Rot and mold.
How many months
Before I'm cold?

Unicorn, sphinx,
    Phoenix, griffin.
How many hours
    Before I stiffen?

Helga, Olga,
    Astrid, Ingrid.
How many days
    Until I'm rigid?

The New York Times,
    Le Monde, Der Sturm.
How many breaths
    Before the worm?

After the Prom

They parked where others parked and steamed
    The windows while they took
Their clothes off just as they had dreamed
    Or read of in a book.

That paradise of pubic hair!
    Those nipples hard and pink!
Swelling with lust, enthralled to stare,
    They briefly paused to think

Of parents, preachers, pregnancy,
    And punishment. In shame,
They looked upon their nudity.
    They looked, they frotted, they came.

Creative Writing

Translating Virgil, eighty lines a day,
Keats never did pick up his MFA.

The Pursuit of Poetry

Les vatiphages me mangent!

—Stéphane Mallarmé

Kevin e-mailed me, eager to "share" his new sestina,
and the flame in the fireplace expired, the temperature
dropped from a hundred to zero, the oil furnace
rumbled in the cellar—in July, in West Palm Beach,
in a house without fireplace, cellar, or furnace.

When Stacey called happily, from her "Poetry House,"
to invite my attendance at an open mike, I watched
color drain from my hand as if it were sculpted in snow.
Then the fist and the telephone became transparent
and no-color drained down the wire into the wall.

At the Antarctic Comfort Inn, after the poetry reading,
"Donald Hall" declined to become *hors d'oeuvres*

in the lobby of poet-eaters. They outfitted my body
in an orange jumpsuit, strapped me to a metal gurney,
and executed me by injecting 500 cc of frigid adulation.

II

RIC'S

PROGRESS

Ric's Progress

1

They met in a bar off campus, where her girlfriend
brought Lucinda to hear the country music jukebox,
and Ric Johnson drank Pickwick with friends. After a dozen
rounds of strong ale, in the parking lot Ric touched Lucinda
where no one had touched her before. In a response
her mother had suggested—providing Ric an anecdote
of their first meeting that he later recounted with tenderness
and pride—Lucinda began their relationship by kicking
Ric where it counted.

2

Lucinda, sometimes Luke or Lucky,
was twenty for the wedding, and Ric was twenty-two.
Luke was *gamine,* aka cute, five foot one in heels,
with a West Texas accent charming in Ric's Boston,
while Ric uprose his suburban generation's six foot two.
Encouraged by her curiosity, Ric permitted Luke
to believe that his amatory experience

was extensive, varied, and expert. Lovemaking
before they married was adventurous—like every
procedure that the late fifties denied to adolescence
and permitted to youth—but collapsed into boredom
with marriage. Ric liked to come twice a day, his practice
when he'd lived alone. Fucking Lucinda was more solitary.
She lay on her back, thoughtful and patient.
"Are you over, honey? Done now, dear?" Their child
suspended loneliness for one year. "Look at what Paulie's
doing! He looks *just* like you!" Then their double resentment
returned doubled. Nothing—not lingual or digital
massage, not long delay or Karezza, not every
procedure recommended by van de Velde, not consultations
with counselors and old roommates, not an Atlantic of tears—
helped. When Ric woke in the night, having fallen asleep
after sex, Lucinda lay awake reading *Bonjour Tristesse* again,
and once she was crying—only nothing was the matter.
Of course Lucky sometimes *liked* it; sometimes
it was really nice, like a head rub.

3

Why did they marry?
Why is it anybody marries anybody?
Because a traffic light changed when it did; because one
morning it rained when it was supposed to snow; because
a friend cherished Roy Acuff; because we understand
that if we ever fully attain what we desire,
we will surely die. Ric Johnson loved saxophones
and tall girls. He married a small woman who hated jazz.
For Lucinda, Ric was a sophisticated alternative
to finishing college. And he *asked* her; nice girls did
what men wanted.

4

Ric liked visiting his in-laws in Texas.
He joked with Bessie, who flirted gaily back at him,
and every morning Buddy drove Ric around the ranch
to check on the horses or washouts after rain.
They drank beer an hour before lunch. After long naps,

they rode Buddy's pintos through acres of tumbleweed,
then drank bourbon two hours before the girl served dinner.
Once, driving in the morning in the gold Cadillac,
Buddy slammed on the brakes to avoid hitting a javelina
and two empty Smirnoff bottles rolled from under his seat,
clanking together. Buddy looked puzzled. "Now how did
they get there?"

5

Ric flew to Chicago for a sales meeting
every first Tuesday, staying with his brother-in-law.
Sometimes he brought a woman. Sometimes Mike fixed him up
with his new girlfriend's roommate, if she was pretty and agreeable,
and they double-dated in Old Town—chile rellenos, Dos Equis,
jokes, and kisses. Ric believed that doing what you want
is virtuous. But what do you *want?* Are you sure it's *this?*
At first Ric supposed that numerousness and secrecy
were aphrodisiac. Many years later he understood:
Betrayal was pleasure enough.

6

Ric's family knew
for a fact that when his great-grandfather had a stroke
in his sixties, two women strange to the family
glared at each other across the open coffin
while his widow sobbed. Then Ric's grandfather
vanished for weekends and returned without excuses
or explanations, permitting Ric's grandmother
to search the Packard for hairpins and earrings.
She wept and blamed the Irish. Ric's father
favored the maid his mother hired from the orphanage
for five dollars a week to assume a black uniform
with a white apron when his mother's best friends
(wearing white gloves and silk dresses, wearing hats
with navy veils) dropped by for bridge, cake, and coffee
on a Thursday afternoon. When Ric's father turned maudlin
after three gins, he called it the Curse of the Johnsons.

7

Ric and Lucky in the orthodox mid-sixties inhabited
an eternal suburb. The sun hung without moving
in the West Newton sky; no one actually died.
After tennis they partied with cocktails. Ric drank Scotch
like everyone, gossiped, danced, and admired the pretty
wives of busy husbands. With their childbearing finished,
children in school all day, they had performed the scripts
their upbringing wrote for them. How to consume the years
left to live? There's the book club. There's Updike and Capote.
There's yoga. But what should they do with their afternoons,
their faces and days? For some, adultery
peppered the casserole cookery of middle youth.
Or at least it plotted the day; or at least its danger
and sport attested: *We are alive.*

8

For ten years,
maturing alcoholics use regular drinking

to demonstrate their control. Then the booze takes over.
So it goes with the habitual adulterer:
He fools around casually for years, or she does,
with predictable pleasure in an absorbing pastime,
and then one day falls in love: catastrophe!
When Twosie—she was a second child—moved into town
with Stephen her husband and the usual children,
Ric chased her like all the men. She was beautiful
enough, blond, with a pretty face, slim hips,
disproportionate breasts, small waist. Twosie
smiled at Ric as she smiled at the others, refusing because
she was used to refusing. But when she looked at herself
after a shower, she saw flesh that began to sag.
Was her life over, before anything interesting happened?
One Saturday at a party they contrived to meet
in a white Formica kitchen. Their mouths opened; their
tongues frolicked. Negotiations commenced
beside a pop-up toaster for their first rendezvous
at a tavern in the country, where they undertook

assignations of an afternoon: pulses rising,
wild breath, astonishing nakedness.

9

Twosie and Ric
rented an apartment in Cambridge—bedroom, kitchen,
and bath—a love nest, tabloids would call it.
For the middle of each day he endured the rest of his life
—while Luke inhabited the galaxy of the PTA;
while Paul struggled in the planetary wars of boyhood—
changing his work schedule to mornings, evenings,
and Saturdays. He arrived at the apartment at noon, brewed coffee,
and waited, pacing the carpet. After Twosie's children
left for school, she picked up, did dishes, returned phone calls,
made appointments for late in the afternoon,
then drove across town and parked her maroon Chevrolet
in a different space each day. They kissed; they drank coffee;
they ran through their news; they went to bed, drank half a bottle
of red with pâté and crackers, and went to bed again.

When Twosie left, always late and hurrying, for house and children,
for beauty parlor, for drinks before supper, for bridge club
Tuesdays at eight, she returned to a life that persisted.
On Friday nights Ric played poker with buddies
and on Sunday mornings did eighteen with Stephen
—but for Ric, only the covert apartment was *true:*
unearthly furtive paradisal Arcadia
where a shepherd and shepherdess tended a soft flock
in criminal secret.

10

After two years, Ric signed the papers
for the judge. Stephen was Lucinda's lawyer,
and Lucinda was guest of honor at a cocktail party
that Stephen and Twosie gave in honor of her divorce.
That day, Ric and Twosie had sex five times, a record.

11

At dawn the telephone rang in Ric's bachelor pad.
Twosie hadn't slept all night, despite the Nembutal.

She was sorry they couldn't fly to New York that day—
but she was certain Stephen would find out everything.
Ric argued calmly: "When we're on the shuttle, you'll feel better."
Twosie was stubborn; Ric turned sarcastic: "I leave
my family; you renege on a dirty weekend."
"Please don't, Ric," she said. She sounded irritable,
which enraged Ric, who shouted—so that Twosie hung up.

In the Combat Zone Ric drank Molson's by the pitcher
all morning. At noon he ate a hamburger and drove
to the secret flat, where he chugalugged half-bottles
until five, when he moved to the Ritz Bar. At midnight,
as he circled toward his Citation, two policemen
suggested that he might forgo driving.
He thanked them for their advice, but after walking
five blocks the cold air cleared his head. They stopped him
driving ten miles an hour with his wheels in the gutter.
Ric slept for the first night of his life on a jail's cement floor,
twitching with rage.

12

       Reconciliation was intense
and brief. When she dismissed him the seventh time,
Ric realized that Twosie would never leave Stephen.
He took to driving alone for three hours midday
on turnpikes and interstates, seeking unprotected
bridge abutments that provided a straight run, open
sightlines, and at ninety miles an hour were unlikely
to leave him quadriplegic as well as depressed.
His daydream sustained him through loneliness, misery,
hatred, and guilt. One noontime, as Ric examined
his shortlist of sites, he noticed that he wore his seatbelt
and kept his speed between forty-five and fifty. He burst
into tears and laughed — exposed for the fraud that he was.

13

By himself, Ric started at five o'clock, assessing
his degree of drunkenness so that supper — Stouffer's,
or spaghetti left over from Paul's Thursday visit —

reduced stupor enough to permit the joy of another
chemical progress. When he attended a party
he drank soda or tonic, because two drinks required
twelve, required vomiting or passing out in public,
required waking with bruises he couldn't remember
incurring but accounted for later when he heard
the stories. At parties he chatted lightly with friends
before driving home sober at midnight, to address
the day's fifth of Heaven Hill. At three A.M. he dialed
the number; after five rings Stephen's exasperated
sleepy voice said hello. It could have been a client
in trouble.

14

Two months after the last breakup,
Ric woke from his drunken sleep to discover Twosie
standing above him in her muskrat coat, shaking him
and smiling through darkness. "No!" he heard himself shouting.
"You never lock your back door," she said as she pulled down

42

her bluejeans. "I'm staying," she told him. "It's arranged.
I told Stephen. We get the children. Shut up."
She sat on him briefly, napped, then left at six A.M.,
as she told him, to fix school lunches and pack her bags.
And that was the end of that.

15

Half a year later,
he trashed her house when Twosie, Stephen, and the children
flew to Switzerland in March for a week of skiing.
Two years before, he had borrowed her house key for a chore
and copied it at a hardware store—in case something happened.
Wearing gloves and galoshes, carrying a knife
and a brick, at midnight, he slipped into the familiar
hallway. Ecstatic, terrified, his heart beat as quick
as a lover's while he slashed the Dali, dented a tea-set,
and shattered the Waterford. The next day, Ric deposited
his burglar tools at a rest area in the country. Returning,
he saw a police car parked at her house, revolving

its blue light. Rapture rushed in his veins, like
the remembered surge and swoon.

16

Undying love dies fast,
and even deathless revenge becomes terminal.
Ric worked to achieve a prophylactic promiscuity:
If love is the source of misery, hysteria, and rage,
maybe many loves, preventing love, permitted calm.
He lived a literary French farce convention
of bedrooms with the doors to each closet or hallway
shut—and unhappy wives behind each door. The lovers
assured each other, while they rubbed and groaned,
that they found hilarious gaiety together
by faking orgasm. When Ric woke beside some weeping
unwelcome stranger, he remembered how Lucinda
wept in her blue Arctic solitude—untouchable,
unable to be touched, touching absolute zero
after seven winters of marriage. Antarctica's

opposite pole, Ric decided with Heraclitus,
produces equivalent cold.

17

To end the story,
Ric's progress delivered him to a Ramada Inn
with a half-gallon of vodka and an assortment of pills.
Why not? His parents were dead; he no longer performed
as a father. (Lucinda married an Anglican vicar
and settled in coastal Essex with Paul, who prepared
for Westminster.) Ric turned on the television set,
sipping and swallowing, trying not to acknowledge
what he was doing, trying to concentrate on plot,
and fell asleep during the episode when Hogan
convinces Colonel Klink that Marlene Dietrich
loves him in secret.

18

After he woke tubed and restrained
in the hospital, he did what the doctor ordered.

He saw Dr. Belle Gaye three times a week — who never
answered his questions, who was unimpressed by drunken
driving, sexual numbers, and psychological cant.
Portions of his rage dwindled, ready to dwindle.
When he remembered his marriage, he understood
that we divorce for the same reasons that we marry,
and we seduce the executioner when we require
to be hanged. On the couch, Ric sagely portrayed himself
as an Oedipal case history, avid for sex
but frightened, who married someone as small as a boy.
(Named Luke.) Dr. Belle Gaye wagged skeptical eyebrows.
When you learn that you've mistaken your feelings
for their opposites — the torturer obsessed by convictions
of disinterested devotion to justice; the suicidal
depressive relentless in cheerfulness — how
can you hope to achieve a deliberate or reasonable life?
How do you keep from repeating the same deceptions
under new disguises? Dr. Belle Gaye never told him.

19

Ric kept his carousel revolving, one old girlfriend
each weekday, weekends reserved for tryouts.
One Sunday he met Molly at a jazz concert.
She was a nurse, randy and humorous, good-looking,
cautious after two marriages, determined to enjoy
her body without the distractions of emotion.
They agreed to pleasure each other without romance,
making an arrangement out of friendship and coming.
They went to movies together; they read the same novels;
they took turns cooking and washing dishes; they took turns
rubbing each other's backs and having head colds.
After a year Ric noticed, with sudden anxiety,
that his set of partners had diminished to Molly.

20

Twenty years later, middle-aged, content and faithful,
settled into a small town north of Seattle, Ric and Molly
made love every day, before Molly did her night shift.

These days, Ric counseled at a recovery center.
Weekends, he and Molly worked in the garden
and walked in mild rain looking for mushrooms. Paul visited
from Vancouver; Ric improvised on an alto saxophone
Saturdays with a band at a Bellingham tavern;
Molly drove to Seattle for lunch with old friends.
Of course they had troubles; everybody has troubles:
They had run low on money; someone got sick or laid off;
the doctor said, "I don't like the look of that blood count."
At some point, one of them would die, then the other.

During their *folie à deux* of friendly endorphins,
they each discovered, independent of the other,
—and then compared notes, startled to arrive together
at the same place at the same time, outside a bedroom—
to be industrious, sober, and monogamous
doesn't *deny life,* as Ric's platitude once had it,
but denies lethargy, vomit, and yeast infections. Love

is permissible — like work, like sexual joy without lying:
the concert of familiar bodies.

21

But never attend
to happy endings — because if stories are happy,
they haven't ended. As Ric and Molly approach sixty,
their skin slackens and wrinkles. He is bald and puffy,
her breasts hang. Touching each other, they take their clothes off.
Does it embarrass or offend you, this nakedness
of people no longer young and smooth-skinned?
One dampens while the other enlarges: They move
to the decaying body's music which is their measure.

1985–2010

III

ROCKING CHAIRS
PAINTED GREEN

The Number

Carolyn telephoned from Ohio to tell me:
"Turn on your TV. Turn on any channel."
The first thing I saw was the second plane
plunging into the south tower over and over.

Turn on your TV. Turn on any channel.
I saw small people jump holding hands
plunging from the south tower over and over.
The whole world watched them falling.

I saw small people jump holding hands
and understood that all of us would perish.
The whole world watched them falling
through smoke that rose in September's air.

I understood that all of us would perish
as I sat in horror two hundred miles away
from smoke that rose in September's air.
Leaves turned red on the tips of branches

as I sat in horror two hundred miles away.
Only Ragged Mountain remained permanent
where leaves turned red on the tips of branches
at the start of the terrifying millennium.

Only Ragged Mountain remained permanent.
I thought of cities without food or succor
at the start of the terrifying millennium.
Who could look away from the fire and dying,

thinking of cities without food or succor?
Carolyn telephoned from Ohio to tell me.
Who could look away from the fire and dying?
The first thing I saw was the second plane.

Scar Tissue

In Montana, that year in the foothills,
her mother breast-fed her to the cup

as I watched with unmitigated joy
through the best year of the marriage.

When she was four, I tickled her ribs
at bedtime, as she laughed requesting

"unnecessary roughness," words
overheard from television football.

She was eight when I left her in divorce.
She insisted on inspecting my shabby

new apartment, and consoled me,
skipping over worn linoleum: "It's *cozy.*"

When she was forty-nine, surgeons
cut into her. Then they cut her again.

Sleep

The engine
of exhaustion
decelerates
slowly, pulling
its eighteen
wheels up
the mountain
as I lie twisted
on my feather
bed. The truck
rattles, whines,
downshifts
metal on metal,
obdurate
in its pitted skin,
while I long for
stupor, my body
ticking a dirge
of stoppage.

Closing

1. "Always Be Closing," Liam told us—
ABC of real estate, used cars,
and poetry. Liam the dandy
loved Brooks Brothers shirts, double-breasted
suits, bespoke shoes, and linen jackets.
On the day Liam and Tree married
in our backyard, Liam and I wore
Chuck's burgundy boho-prep high-tops
that Liam bought on Fifth Avenue.

2. When the rain started, we moved indoors
and Liam read a Quartet aloud.
T. S. Eliot turned old and frail
at sixty, pale, preparing for death.
Then poets of new generations
died—Frank O'Hara first, then Jim Wright
with throat cancer in a Bronx hospice,
Sylvia Plath beside the oven,
Thom Gunn of an overdose, Denise

3. Levertov, Bob Creeley, Jane Kenyon . . .
In a New York bar, Liam told me
eccentric, affectionate stories
about a road trip in Tree's country
of Montana, and the joy they felt
in the abundance of their marriage.
At Bennington Tree said, "Fourteen years
after the wedding in your backyard,
I love Liam with my entire heart."

4. Liam's face changed quickly as he spoke,
eyes and mouth erupting with gusto
as he improvised his outrageous,
cheerful, inventive obscenities.
When I first met him—I expounded
at a young poet's do—his bearded
face was handsome and expressionless.
He would not defer to a poet
fifty years old! After a few months

5. he was revising my lines for me,
making the metaphors I couldn't.
Even now, working at poems, I
imagine for a moment Liam
disassembling them. A year ago
he watched the progress of age turn me
skeletal, pale flesh hanging loosely
in folds from my arms, and thin rib bones
like grates above a sagging belly.

6. His body would never resemble
my body. Four or five times a week
we wrote letters back and forth, talking
about class structure, about how Tree
took charge over the Academy
of American Poets, about
poems and new attacks on free speech . . .
When I won a notorious prize,
Liam sent me eighty-one notions

7. about projects I might undertake.
Number fifty-six instructed me:
"Urge poets to commit suicide."
His whole life he spoke of suicide
lightly, when he wasn't preserving
the First Amendment from Jesse Helms,
or enduring two colon cancers,
or watching films, or chatting with Tree,
or undergoing heart surgeries.

8. If he walked their dog Keeper one block,
he had to take nitroglycerin.
When Jane was dying, Liam and Tree
drove up to say goodbye. I wheelchaired
Jane to a pile of books on the floor
to find the color plate of Caillebotte's
shadowy kitchen garden at Yerres
for the jacket of *Otherwise,* when
Tree would design it. I think of Jane's

9. horror if she were alive to know
that on August fifteenth Liam pulled
the shotgun's trigger. The night before,
wearing a tux over a yellow
silk shirt, he danced with Tree once again,
before bed and the morning's murder.
He left Tree alone and desolate
but without anger. Tree knew Liam
did what he planned and needed to do.

What We Did

Early each morning I rose to bring you coffee in bed.
You kindled a woodfire in your workroom above the kitchen,
then walked Gus up-mountain for half an hour.
When you returned, you climbed upstairs to a warm desk

at the house's southeast corner. I sat below and away,
on the ground floor, and we wrote poems together.
If we met in the kitchen, pouring another cup of coffee,
we never broke silence. We patted bluejeaned bottoms.

For lunch we made sandwiches and chatted lightly.
We lay down for a twenty-minute nap, and woke to fuck,
dallying twisted together. Then I read aloud for an hour
from a writer we loved—Henry James, Keats, Bishop . . .

You cooked dinner, sipping from a glass of white wine.
I drank my beer looking at the latest *New Yorker.*
We ate by candlelight at the table, then read together
in our armchairs in silence under separate cones of light.

Searching

We grieve that Jane's away.
I know she's dead—but Gus is
Never so sure. Today
    He mopes and fusses,

And when we're back from walking
He sniffs at her armchair
And listens for her talking,
    And climbs the stair

To poke an inquiring nose
Under a hamper's lid,
For Jane, he must suppose,
    Returned and hid.

The Gardener

Into your mid-forties you tended
your flowers each day of spring:
sweet mayflowers like late snow
underfoot, red poppies, snowdrops,
fiddlehead ferns, lilacs purpling,
trilliums, apparition of daffodils,
bridal veil spireas, lady's slippers,
ragged eruption of forsythia,
lilies of the valley, wild foxglove . . .

You would have turned sixty today.

The Offspring

One morning, suddenly overwhelmed,
Jane hurled me on the sofa, her lust
reciprocated without precaution.
She missed her period. In daydream,
I happily held and changed a newborn—
but Jane had known since her teens
that she should not bear a child.
When she bled a month later, I booked
an appointment with the surgeon
we called Dr. Snip-snip. After Jane died,
I kept imagining the composite face
of an adolescent who was not here—
black-haired, motherless, despondent.

Freezes and Junes

She laid bricks arranged
in V's underneath

the garden's rage of blossom.
After her death, after

the freezes of many winters,
her bricks rise and dip

undulant by the wellhead,
in summer softened by moss,

and in deep June I see
preterite, revenant poppies

fix, waver, fix, waver, fix . . .

The Widower's Cowbell

Pay attention, please, to how pitiable I am,
a forlorn cow who has lost her cowbell, in pastures
I would like to call the Pastures of Melancholy,
only people might think I felt sorry for myself.
Put down this sad, appealing poem
and come with me to the graveyard
to watch me wearing sackcloth, tailored and tapered,
with a dash of ash on my aging cheeks
while a video camera disguised as a yew tree
records my performance of charming grief.
Try reading me again tomorrow
when I wake up mournful in my black pajamas
looking forward to Grape-Nuts Flakes and ululation.

Blue Snow

Pete Sullivan dropped by:
"Your barn needs work, and so do I."
Pete had the eye

To fix old boards with new
And keep the handy knotholes through
Which swallows flew.

Pete raked and scraped away
Seventy-year-old scraps of hay
And found the sleigh

That frisky Riley drew
In nineteen hundred thirty-two
When snow fell blue.

Old cowbarns tilt awry
When sills go punky, and that's why
Peter dropped by.

Goosefeathers

When I was twelve I sat by myself in the steamliner
with a shoebox of sandwiches and deviled eggs
my mother made, and ate everything right away
as the train headed north by the Sound where trestles
of derelict trolley lines roosted nations of seagulls.
From South Station I took a taxi across Boston
to a shabby, black locomotive with coal car
that pulled two rickety coaches. It puffed past
long lines of empty commuter trains, past
suburbs thick with houses, past the milltowns
of Lawrence and Lowell, until the track curved
into New Hampshire's pastures of Holstein cattle.
My grandfather waited in his overalls at the depot
with horse and buggy to carry me to the farmhouse,
to fricasseed chicken, corn on the cob, and potatoes.
At nine o'clock, after shutting up the chickens
from skunk and fox, we sat by the cabinet radio
for Gabriel Heatter booming news of the war.
I slept through the night on my goosefeather bed.

The Back Chamber

Here is the house's genius: pram and bedstead,
       Heart-shaped Valentine candy
   Boxes, oil lamps, a captain's chair,
   And Ben Keneston's underwear,
     A century ago
Folded away in case it came in handy,
       By prudent family dead.

Here chests keep layers of relics: a beaded purse,
       A graduation dress
    That Ben's wife Lucy made in homespun,
    Reports from school in nineteen-one,
     A century ago,
And painted China heads, now bodiless,
      From dolls of three dead daughters.

Maples

When I visited as a boy, too young for chores,
a pair of maples flared before the farmhouse.
My grandfather made me a swing, dangling
rope from stout branches. I hurtled
between them high as I could, pumping
out half the day while my mind daydreamed
the joy of no school, no camp, no blocks
of other children fighting childhood's wars.
With the old people I listened to radio news
of Japanese in Nanking, Madrid on fire,
Hitler's brownshirts *heiling*. The hurricane
of 1938 ripped down the older maple.

When I was twelve and could work the fields,
my grandfather and I, with Riley the horse,
took four days to clear the acres of hay
from the fields on both sides of the house.
With a scythe I trimmed the uncut grass
around boulders and trees, by stone walls,

and raked every blade to one of Riley's piles.
My grandfather pitched hay onto the wagon
where I climbed to load it, fitting it tight.
We left the fields behind as neat as lawns.
When I moved back to the house at forty,
a neighbor's machine took alfalfa down
in an afternoon. Next morning, engines
with huge claws grappled round green bales
onto trucks, leaving loose hay scattered
and grass standing at the field's margin.

A solitary maple still rises. Seventy years
after my grandfather hung the swing,
maple branches snap from the old tree.
I tear out dead limbs for next year's sake,
fearing the wind and ice storms of winter,
fearing broken trees, cities, and hipbones.

The Bone Ring

The summer when I saw the Trylon and Perisphere,
I sat on the farm porch with my great-uncle Luther,
who told me that when he was nine he watched
the soldier boys walking back home from Virginia.

Then the new war started, and always another war.

He showed me family keepsakes from the attic—
a top hat his father wore, a bugle, and remnants
that emptied the pockets of a cousin killed at Shiloh:
a button, a spoon, and a ring carved out of bone.

Alterations

My great-grandfather built the woodshed in 1865,
cobbled together from clapboard, with enough space
for a five-holed outhouse and worn farm equipment.
In middle age, when I moved here to stay
and snowdrifts piled tall in the yard, I carried
kindling and firewood, without stepping outside,
from shed through toolshed to kitchen range
and Glenwood parlor stove. After a dozen years
of hauling, I gave up and installed an oil furnace.

The woodshed became a museum of rusted scythes.
Now that old age prospers, walking to the car
over the driveway's ice can break your head. So
I hired a carpenter's crew to expand the woodshed
into a garage with an electric door opening from inside,
as tidy and decorative as suburban Long Island.
No wonder that I backed out one afternoon
without raising the door, smashing it to pieces
like an idiot, like a man speeding into his eightieth year.

Pieces

Now I am eighty years old, content to sit in my chair
watching unpainted boards of the barn
turn amber when late autumn sun rubs against them.

It is the same barn I ran to as a ten-year-old
to sit on a three-legged stool beside my grandfather
while he milked his seven Holsteins and spoke
pieces he learned for school: "Lawyer Blue,"
"The Bearded Hen," "An Orphan Lad from Boston."
He recited a version of "Casey at the Bat"
where Casey hits a home run, because my grandfather
couldn't bear to say that Casey had struck out.

If he saw me now, would he need to turn away?
Or would he laugh, and remember another piece,
"The Sly Old Farmer Outsmarts the Drummer"?

Envy

Ambitious in middle life, I envied her simple, unambiguous joy.
When she was young, she chased her slobbery tennis ball
and carried it back to me, teasing, or leapt two feet in the air
in ecstasy at my morning return from buying the newspaper,
or, instinct with rapture, hurtled through first snow
to explode a smoke of powder from her paws, or walking
vanished into the summer woods, then panted waiting
by a birch on New Canada Road she knew I would come to.

A dozen years later her hindquarters dragged and twisted,
or her legs splayed on linoleum as she bent to eat
from her bowl of kibble, or she struggled to curve her back
in order to defecate, and shit accumulated in her fur, until
one night she crawled on the floor in spasms like a seal
flippering on sand. The next morning, with dread and resolve,
I drove her to the veterinarian, whose needle killed her.
In painful old age, I envy the instant mercy of pentobarbital.

"Poetry and Ambition"

He sits to pick at lines that try to become a poem
in the Morris chair his mother and father gave him
when he wrote after school with his bedroom door shut.

At fourteen he resolved to become an immortal poet.
In middle age he won prizes, honors, fellowships,
and read his poems at colleges hundreds of times.

Then it stopped. The anthologies dropped him out.
Poetry festivals never invited him. An octogenarian
sits in the blond maple chair writing, crossing out,

picking up a thesaurus, trying to find a metaphor—
and makes a doddery language with no poetry in it.
If no one will ever read him again, what the fuck?

Green Farmhouse Chairs

1. In the back chamber, discarded things
of family jumble together,
nothing thrown away since we moved here
in eighteen sixty-five. I foresee
an auction of broken rocking chairs
painted farmhouse green, thick wooden skis,
oil lamps, my great-grandfather's flannel
nightshirts, stacks of *Youth's Companion,* lasts
for resoling shoes, toys, eight stacked beds . . .

2. I know you don't listen, Kurt Schwitters,
but pitchers and catchers drive their cars
south in February, while Fenway's
baseball lies under snow. You collect
yourself in the framed, deep-set collage
Linda and I discovered at Yale.
Idolatrous of this white farmhouse
since I was ten, in my ninth decade
I daydream that it burns to the ground

3. so that nobody will empty it.
My children comfort me with their care,
bringing five grandchildren to visit,
but none will settle in the country.
When I was twelve and we didn't hay,
Kurt, the parlor radio broadcast
the Red Sox games. As Henry Moore carved
or modeled his sculpture every day,
he strived to surpass Donatello

4. and failed, but awoke the next morning
elated for another try. At
eighty-five he dozed in a wheelchair.
I list the objects of this long house,
walking from room to room taking notes,
as if I control or determine
what happens to things after I die.
In June the peonies go rotten
and white old roses flourish briefly.

5. This wooden box beside my blue chair
was built by a cabinetmaker
to hold the toys of his first grandson,
my father, who died at fifty-two.
Inside it are LPs of poets,
dead and reading their work with gusto.
Let them melt. Baseball will inflate, Kurt,
into yearlong seasons under domes.
My mother made it until ninety.

6. All day I sit silent and alone
watching the barn or TV baseball,
usually grateful for the hours
of isolation's slow contentment—
but I long for days when Linda comes.
I ask, "What will you do when I die?"
"I will sit in a chair for two years."
My grandchildren's grandchildren will know
nothing of a grassy cellar hole.

7. Linda gave me the book *Kurt Schwitters,*
with murky photos from the twenties
of your Merzbaus, and of collages
footnoted as "whereabouts unknown."
Hitler's war and our bombing wasted
Hamburg, where your rash and bountiful
inventions burnt into ash. I think
of the lost Red Sox I read about
in the *Boston Post:* Babe Ruth long gone,

8. Ted Williams, Mel Parnell, Bobby Doerr,
Birdie Tebbetts . . . My wife Jane Kenyon
died at forty-seven, no longer
able to write. I imagine her
at sixty, outliving hot flashes,
writing in depression new poems
about an old man who cannot fuck.
She looks after him as he shuffles
into a bent and shriveled other.

9. Like all shelters, Kurt—huts and mansions—
this house built two centuries ago
contained its end in its beginning,
in its anvil-forged spikes and timbers.
Benjamin Keneston, Aunt Nannie,
and Wesley Wells are dead. After hours
of Cheyne-Stokes breathing they went silent,
as useless and beyond self-pity
as broken rocking chairs painted green.